Liminal

Brenda Eldridge

Liminal

Liminal
ISBN 978 1 76109 341 8
Copyright © text Brenda Eldridge 2022
Cover image: Pat Whelen on Unsplash

First published 2022 by
GINNINDERRA PRESS
PO Box 3461 Port Adelaide 5015
www.ginninderrapress.com.au

Contents

Introduction	7
Slipping Through the Cracks	9
A Door Opening	13
Life and Death	14
Wise Woman	22
Links	31
Cultures	38
Home Studies and Ginninderra Press	42
Who am I?	46

Introduction

I have been reluctant to write of these things. I have said for years I write to make things real and it's been as if by putting anything into words on a page it leaves me – I can somehow separate myself from those events or feelings. But it also makes them real so they can't be denied. I don't know if I am writing now to free myself or to embrace myself. And I'm not sure if, or how much, I want to know the answer to that.

Where to start? One morning, I gave up trying to get back to sleep. I had drifted since five, when it was too early to get up. So I waited till nearer six, when I quietly slipped out of bed hoping not to disturb my sleeping Stephen, and took my clothes from the chair, remembering to pick up my glasses. Instead of going straight into the bathroom, I went into the spare bedroom to look out of the east-facing window to see what the sky was doing.

No brilliant display of pink clouds, but lots of grey ones. I looked up and saw Venus and Jupiter, as I have been doing lately – and there she was! The moon. Only a small sickle, she will be visible for another morning, possibly two, before we go into the dark quarter. I took an involuntary breath in surprise. I whispered 'My lady' and hugged myself in delight that I had seen her – and went off to have a shower.

The question is, how did I become a seventy-two-year-old woman, mother, grandmother, great-grandmother, wife, stepmother, editor, poet, essayist, artist and friend who ends every single day sending her prayers of thanks to the moon?

Slipping Through the Cracks

I have had an amazing life and have written about a lot of it over the years, starting when I was thirty-three and my dad died. Currently, I have been trying to write a book called *Right Time and Right Place*. I wanted it to be like a bookend. *Flower Child* was about my first eleven years. *Right Time and Right Place* is intended to be about the last thirteen years since sharing my life with Stephen.

These later years have been the healing time for those between the ages of eleven and fifty-nine. It will make an interesting story if I ever finish doing it. But while I can write about the facts, even about discovering in Stephen I have a like-minded soul for my life partner, I know that I am still an individual with my own thoughts, feelings and beliefs. Things I have been reluctant to talk about much because I didn't want them to be mocked or ridiculed. I had more than enough of that in my first marriage to make me very cautious.

*

Growing up in the heart of the English countryside, my life was not impinged upon by the norms of suburbia. I slipped through the cracks. I read that sentence again because it makes me smile. My world as written about in *Flower Child* was reality for me. I wonder now if it was something I created, like the imaginary friends of a lonely child. That is the voice of logic and reason, the voice that I will try and give little space to as I write – other than to acknowledge it exists. One of my brothers read *Flower Child* and said, while he remembered different things, essentially what I had written about was accurate.

This is about my world, how it evolved with my own awareness of things.

Mother encouraged me by talking about the flower fairies. The Flower Fairy books were written and illustrated by Cicely Mary Barker. I was so familiar with those plants and trees and there was, and still is, no doubt in my mind that the fairies were there in the garden and wayside. It didn't occur to me to doubt her or them. They were my company as I played in my own utterly safe world, I was happy in the orchards, woods and meadows. The flowers were my friends. Perhaps Mother too had been a lonely child and she needed them for comfort and company. I will never know.

I have yearned for her attention all of my life. She told me I cried for the first two years. All I wanted was a cuddle. She was swamped by the needs of husband and two small sons in a time when life in post-war England was hard for everyone. She married not knowing how to cook or run a home. How frightened she must have been to be pregnant, learning how to look after her babies, create a home in a centuries-old house and with very little money.

I recall when I was about thirty I attended a two-day study course. Among other things, we did a meditation that took us to a time before being born into this life. I knew without a shadow of a doubt that I was wanted. Perhaps I didn't get the hugs I so badly needed. I tried so hard to be like my brothers so I would get my parents' attention. Mother gifted me the flower fairies instead. I don't remember being lonely. Solitary always but not lonely.

*

I already knew I was different at primary school. I didn't make friends. In the last two years, I was alone there as my older brothers had left and gone on to secondary school. Without their protection, I was the subject of bullying.

My instincts told me not to talk of flower fairies or the ghosts of Roman soldiers who lived in the house and in the woods surrounding the village. I wasn't afraid of the soldiers but I was wary. I acknowledged their presence and carried on.

Two years after my dad died, I returned to the farmhouse for a few weeks. I took with me a gift for Mother. It was a set of wind chimes consisting of one hundred small brass bells. My brother fixed it to the wall of the house outside our mother's bedroom window. The chimes drove the ghost from the house. It had felt odd without Dad there but it was the absence of the ghost that was the biggest change. He came to me one night. I felt him trying to suffocate me. I fought him off and he was gone. The house felt empty after that.

*

As I wrote in *Flower Child*, I knew as a child that I didn't connect with even the gentle influence of the local church. There was no special feeling when I was inside the building, even though it was a thousand years old. I have thought since about all those prayers over the centuries and once, on a peaceful sunny afternoon with birdsong filling the air, it was easy to feel the devotion of so many over the centuries.

Going to Sunday school and the Sunday morning service were part of ordinary childhood for me and my brothers. We lived in a farming community, so harvest thanksgiving services had special significance. It was a natural feeling to want to give thanks for home, health and food. 'We plough the fields and scatter, the good seed on the land' are the opening lines to a hymn I have loved since childhood. It goes on, 'but it is fed and watered by God's almighty hand…'

It would have been easier for me perhaps if I could have accepted the idea of an almighty God, but I didn't. I couldn't make a connection between 'an almighty God' and nature doing what nature does every moment – the constant balancing of cause and effect and life lusting after life.

Even back then, I couldn't accept the very foundation of the Christian belief system. As a teenager, I remember thinking that if there was a person called Jesus, then what he seemed to have dedicated his life to had very little in common with the organised Christian religion I had been exposed to both in fact and in history lessons.

I lived in Ireland briefly when I was nineteen/twenty and saw first hand the hypocrisy and fear in people's lives because of the Catholic church. My children's father was an Irish Catholic and while he had no interest in churchgoing, when our children were born he was adamant that they be baptised. I had no objection but found it bewildering that he found it so hard to find a Catholic priest to baptise our children because I was English and not a Catholic. I was very naive and unworldly then.

In my early twenties here in Australia, our eldest son turned five or six. It was time to consider him making his first holy communion at aged seven. I didn't want my child frightened like the children I met in Ireland, and what appeared to be lingering in his father, and embarked on learning more about it for myself.

Loneliness drew me to the warmth of some Jesuit priests and Catholic nuns. I became a Catholic but, much as I longed to feel I belonged to the congregation, I knew in my heart I simply didn't. After a while, I walked away carefully as I didn't want to hurt or offend the people who had shown me kindness.

Some years later, my second son took his own life. I only vaguely knew that the church's view of suicides – that they were trapped in some state called purgatory for eternity – and certainly it was nothing I wanted to entertain at any level for my son.

I remember writing to the local priest not long after my son died and explaining my views and asking him if there was anything I needed to do to cut myself off from the church completely. He was very careful in his response, I still have the letter somewhere. He acknowledged I had clearly given the matter a lot of thought, and there was nothing I needed to do as such, but to ensure that I told my family to prevent any difficulties when I died and someone was arranging my funeral.

Separating myself from the Christian church was not an end to my spiritual development. I was just saying Christianity was not for me.

A Door Opening

I had been home based for seventeen years raising my children and I wanted a year to myself before I joined the work force. I had become a mother when I was barely nineteen. I had no idea who I was, what I wanted from this life. I knew there was more to me than being someone's wife and someone's mother, though my commitment to both was sincere.

By the time I was thirty-five and my youngest child had started school, my marriage was all but over. Enquiries at the local TAFE revealed I only needed to do four subjects instead of five for matriculation. Something in me hungered for more knowledge and I had a barely acknowledged desire to go to university. I thought I needed matriculation in order to follow that path.

Being a full-time student and running a home of six people with no practical help was not possible beyond the first semester, but I did become aware that I knew far more than I realised and I was pleased with my three Bs and a C when, with a heavy heart, I walked away.

I had chosen Classics as one of my subjects and that took me into the world of the ancient Greeks, not only their history but their mythology. It was like coming home. I might not have been able to continue my studies but I didn't stop reading. In fact, my curiosity just sent me further afield. Far removed from the notion of there being one god, the people I was reading about had a whole pantheon of gods.

Life and Death

When I started writing about life and death, I became entangled in the vastness of it all, expecting to be able to tidy things up so they were manageable. Stephen has given me a timely reminder that there will always be things too big to get my mind around. In the past, that has been applied to the hard things. I had forgotten that it applies to the beautiful positive things too. How blessed I am that I don't tire of witnessing sunrises and sunsets, the wonders of the universe and our planet within the universe. And people.

*

I know without the sun there is no life on this planet. I have stood on the beach to watch the sun setting and known that moment of terror as the last tiny glimpse of golden fire disappeared. A couple of times I have even seen that magic flash of electric blue. The burning question was, and still is with each sunset, will it come back?

Small wonder then that I love to watch the sun rise. I love how the sky changes, the gradual brightness… I refer to the sun as the Great Spirit. I see my life as a path to the sun. Not so much a straight line – there have been so many diversions that have taken me wandering to all kinds of places, mentally, physically and spiritually – but always I am on that main path to the sun.

*

I am not going into the details. Suffice it to say that things reached a point in my marriage when I faced death at my husband's hands. I had feared the violence, the cruelty, but in that moment I stopped being afraid. I did not fear death. I don't know if I have been sustained by this or I just stopped caring. On reflection, it was the turning point in my marriage and part of me shut down, withdrawing for self-protection. Death threats made some years later were different and resulted in me actually leaving.

At my lowest ebb, I did contemplate taking my own life, but the hunger for life was too strong. I know I do not want to die but I do not fear death.

*

There are events in everyone's life that make them aware of how solitary we are. Grief at my son taking his own life, the impact it had on my family, recovering from domestic violence isolated me. It took thirty years and an unexpected attack on me as a grieving mother to shock me out of that isolation.

Death of the young shocks us all far more than the death of someone who has lived a long life, regardless of how they lived. When an adult dies, we still grieve according to how important that person was to us, but there is some kind of saving grace in the fact that they lived long enough to have lived their life, known the ups and downs we all experience. Some could say at twenty-one my son was an adult, and perhaps they are correct. He is my son, he will ever be my child. I have been telling my boys since they were teenagers that no matter how old they get, they will always be my babies, my little boys.

Grief changes over time by how much we allow new things and people into our lives. It doesn't go away, but it doesn't have to block other things out.

Suicide is very distressing to any lives that are touched by it. It's made worse by a general consensus that it shouldn't be talked about. I think we all have difficulty accepting this ultimate rejection of us as people. It must make us take notice of what our society has become. There must be that flood of questions: why did it happen, what could have been done to prevent it? Every time someone takes their own life, we are all responsible.

*

When my son took his own life, I felt my arms had been pulled from their sockets. For thirty-one years, I have had bleeding stumps not arms. But I must qualify that. It was the arms that could hold the child that was gone, not the arms that could hold others. Not so much these days, but for years I have hugged myself when distressed about what happened, as if I could stop the agony by holding my arms back on, except of course that could not happen, he took them with him.

I made a conscious decision immediately after he died that I was not going to hide his life or death. I was going to use it in whatever way I could to enlighten people, make them aware of what they do and say and how it impacts on other lives. I was determined I was going to make his life and death count for something. I refused to let it be a waste. I know my approach was challenging, and too hard for many, but I was forced by reality to make the choice of what I was going to do next.

I have not questioned the why he chose to die, that was abundantly clear to anyone who witnessed our lives. When I heard the words that he was dead, my first thought was thank goodness he is out of it at last.

It is commonly said that suicide is the act of a coward. I tried putting myself in his position. I imagined myself standing on a precipice. Behind me was my life, all the positives and negatives, all the things and people I knew and cared about. If I stepped over that precipice, I was going into the the unknown.

He did that cold sober – the autopsy showed there were no foreign substances in his body. On a sunny afternoon, he put a gun to his head and pulled the trigger. I didn't know what my son believed in, whether he believed in an afterlife, or a heaven or hell. I can only marvel at his courage or his faith if indeed he had that.

This morning in the shower, I became aware that I am not so different from my son. I am not afraid of what I don't know.

My family will always consider it a tragic waste that one of our number took themselves away, but we are also better people than we might otherwise have been.

*

The Greek mythologies I had started reading some years before my son died had opened my mind to the world of gods and the certainty in that culture of the Underworld watched over by Hades. If you had been a 'good' person, you went to the Elysian Fields, and if you hadn't, you were destined to wander the Underworld – in what the Catholics seem to have adopted and called purgatory.

Written into this, too, is the concept of revenge. It appears that it was believed if someone would not, could not rest in peace because their death had not been avenged, then it was up to those left behind to sort this out.

Revenge is a miserable thing. I certainly understand why people feel this driving need for revenge, to hurt someone as much as they have been hurt, but where does it end? Nothing is ever as simple as an eye for an eye.

*

I have had to accept that I would never know what the life of my children's father was about before we met. The political climate as it was, with our mixed marriage of Irish/English we were not welcome in either country. With our young family in a new country far away from everything familiar, we had a chance to create a way of life of our own choosing. I only wanted our home to be a safe haven. He wanted to be the head of the household, his way or no way. His determination to retain his need to be just that resulted in me being driven out of our home, from my children and from a community. It also resulted in our second son taking his own life. It would seem our son saw no other way of getting away from his domineering father.

Even in the early stages of shock, I worked out that there was nothing I could think of that would hurt my ex-husband enough, so I didn't waste any time or energy on it. I also knew instinctively that I would be hurting myself more than I could ever hurt him.

Nothing I could do, think or say would bring my son back. And I didn't want him to come back. Why would I wish him back if he felt strongly enough to take his own life to get away from what he had here?

*

Karma and reincarnation: we used to call it swings and roundabouts, or what goes around comes around. It still comes down to be careful what you do because it might come back to you. Again, this isn't always a negative thing, Stephen and I often think that somewhere in our youth or childhood, we must have done something good.

I did speculate over the years whether my son had come back in another time, place and body. I certainly did look for traces of him in my grandsons when they were born but, as it turned out, he wasn't obviously visible in them, although I have seen constant reminders of him in his brothers. Until very recently.

I have suddenly become aware that my surviving three sons, now in their forties and fifties, have grown more and more alike with the passing of years. I find this fascinating because when I look at photographs of all of them from long ago, four brothers couldn't look more physically different and they were certainly individuals in their thoughts and behaviour. Now they do look alike but they also talk in a similar way, move in a similar way. And I had to face squarely the expression I have used for years – forever young. They have gone on without him. It was a shocking realisation, though I don't think I was surprised. I know he is still part of who they are. He took his physical body away, he hasn't grown to have a partner, children, but he is still in all of us.

In writing that, I feel the link that nothing can destroy or deny. These men are my sons. I carried them in my body until it was time for them to be born. They are brothers. We are all of the same – what? The quick answer is family, but that doesn't seem to quite cover it.

I'm not one for social media but Stephen has a Facebook page through which I can keep in touch with what my brother and his family in England are doing. I see photographs of him and there is my dad, or my sons looking back at me. The likenesses are uncanny and for me comforting. I see in my brother's grandchildren similarities to our other brother's children. It's like an invisible spiderweb.

Reincarnation: I mean no offence to anyone, but reincarnation seems to be one of those incalculable ideas. It's still making assumptions or blind leaps of faith about what comes after we die. Many years ago, I listened to my ex-husband talk about reincarnation, but it seemed to be as an academic exercise, possible even a ploy to impress. There is no way of knowing. But it has stayed with me. Particularly since my son died.

As I have written often, after he died I carefully looked at all the standards and values that I lived my life by. Who was I? What had I taught my children without being aware of what I had done or said? I wasn't prepared to continue accepting anything just because my parents taught me, or because I had read something somewhere. In amongst all this questioning was an underlying fear that if I didn't get *this* life right, I would have to come back and do it again.

Amazing as my life has been, I'd rather not come back and do it again. Some say we are born wanting to experience certain things. This presupposes some sort of ability for conscious thought before we are actually physically created at the point of conception. So it's not just about what comes after this life, but what came before. We talk of an old head on young shoulders, or someone with an old soul. What are we really saying?

*

As for what happens after we die, I don't know. My dad died when I was thirty-three. I hadn't seen or spoken to him since I left England aged twenty-one. That was only due to the way international communications were in the 1970s and 80s. He left me feeling I had been cast adrift in the universe. At my brothers' insistence, I didn't return to England to see him before he died aged sixty, so my memories of him were and still are of a young man striding about the woods, meadows and orchards where I grew up. He was cremated, so there is no grave to visit and lay flowers upon.

For a couple of months after my son died, I felt I was carrying him in my arms but he was growing heavier by the day. There came a time I knew I needed to lay him down. He had asked to be buried and we honoured that, but this was something different. I did the only thing I could think of: I gave him to my dad. I asked him to look after my son. In my mind's eye, for the past thirty-one years, I have an image of them walking through a beechwood with flickering sunlight coming down through the leaves. They are walking away from me and are in perfect harmony.

Is it strange, I wonder, that I didn't envision my mother joining them when she died just over three years ago, or myself when I die. Trying to accept the fact that I would never see, hear or touch him ever again was one of the hardest things to try and adjust to and my arms will always ache for him. That and the fact there is no child of my child. Even so, I was not tempted to think that one day we would be reunited.

*

I don't know how I feel about forgiveness. I recognised the futility and potential harm that can come from revenge, but forgiveness…

My understanding of forgiveness is to say to someone what you have done is OK. Our son made the decision to go. His decision was absolutely right for him. I have not doubted that for one moment. Rather, I have been in awe that he stayed as long as he did. Three days after he died, he came to me and as clear as day he said, 'It's all right, Mum.' And I knew it was. I have not ever doubted that he is all right.

But we, his parents, were responsible for what happened in the years leading up to that decision. His father tried to control everything our son did. How am I supposed to say to his father it's OK that you drove our son to do what he did?

Just as nothing I could do or say could bring my son back, so I was helpless in trying to change his father. He didn't change even after our son died. He showed the same implacable obduracy.

I find I can talk to my ex-husband in my head and apologise for not being the person he thought I was, or wanted me to be. I do apologise for the hurt I caused him, but I don't need to apologise for being young and naive and having a mind of my own.

*

For years, I have prayed for serenity. I realised not so long ago that it isn't serenity I should strive for but dignity. Will there ever be a time when my heart is not outraged by the death of my son and the attempted destruction of me as the person I was meant to be? I don't know.

I have had so much goodness and positiveness in my life these past few years, I had thought I might have managed this forgiveness notion better. I think it is something I go round and round in circles about. It isn't about understanding someone else. It's accepting that this is who they are.

I have said many times, love me or leave me alone. I say I have done the best I could with what I had on the day. As I insist on this for myself, then I must extend the same to others. I must make a deliberate decision to accept that person did the best they could with what they had on the day.

So it isn't about forgiveness or understanding. It is about acceptance, which I do with varying degrees of success on any day.

Wise Woman

Looking back, I don't know where the idea came from, but I can remember clearly making a statement to an elderly Jesuit priest who I had become friends with. I was in my mid-to-late twenties and I said I wanted to be a wise woman, living in the desert, and people would come to me for what I could give them. It wasn't said out of arrogance and at that time I had no idea how it was to eventuate.

Not long after making that announcement, we moved away from the area and I lost contact with all of the people in my life at that time. I am not one of those people who makes lifelong friends. When the time comes to move on, I go without a backward glance and I prefer not to take anyone with me. A new start meant, and still means, a new start.

*

Going back to those college days in my mid-thirties for a moment and the ancient Greek mythologies. Anthropomorphic – I had a new word, a concept different from what was being offered by Christian beliefs. The ancient Greeks talked about their gods as if they were people like themselves, beings that lived in their daily lives with all the human frailties they had and we have. They didn't hold one single god up above everything, the be-all and end-all. There was a hierarchy, just as in a family, and different members had different roles to play. I find it a delight that Zeus might be the head of that family, but he still had to contend with the challenges from his wife Hera regarding his philandering. Not so easily done!

Gods were respected, feared perhaps but not in the way I had seen in the eyes of some who had grown up in the world of Christian organisations with its teachings of heaven, hell, eternal damnation and a God who knows every thought and sees every deed, thus instilling a terrible sense of guilt about simply being human. I instantly connected with the Greek notion of a pantheon of gods.

*

When I had to give up my formal studies, I went to work in the Department of Social Security (DSS, now Centrelink) and embarked on a new path of discovery. I see now that I was setting forth to find myself. The most important thing about joining the workforce was recognising that it was my opportunity to prove there was more to me than being someone's wife or someone's mother. I was the one creating my reputation and I was determined to prove I was good at what I was doing and I could be relied upon to do my work well.

It started in a very basic way with image. There was no uniform but a dress code of neat and tidy. I opted for the eccentric English woman living overseas look – not quite twinsets, pearls and tweeds but certainly classic rather than trendy. I took to wearing scarves to add what I thought was a touch of elegance. I was also dealing with the public and honed my English speaking voice. I chuckle about it now, but when in a difficult situation, I climbed up on my English dignity and won the respect and caring of work colleagues and clients alike. I suspect I still do it in times of stress or challenge.

It was also then that I started wearing school sandals. I wanted my feet planted firmly on the earth, no high heels business. I was deliberately developing a 'country woman's plod'. I still do only wear sandals, but now I have a range of colours, some with flower and butterfly designs and one pair with dots like an Aboriginal painting.

Was it serendipity that I was blessed that a general trend began then, at least here in Adelaide, of easy access to alternative views. I could go to big department stores and find books on the beliefs and mythologies of many different cultures. I will write of these things not necessarily in the chronological order they came my way.

My reading drifted in a different direction too and, again, I am not writing in the order of books as I came across them. But they were all linked. I was learning about different cultures and different methods of divination and how very important they were to each culture. There was always an acknowledgement of something beyond themselves, a source to be respected, revered and appealed to. Also there was no such thing as a free lunch. There was always a price to pay, and those payments were not necessarily obvious or convenient. This was a world of fantasy and enchantment.

I hadn't seen it until I embarked on this exploration of how I became this woman I am but I used the world of fantasy and enchantment to counter the harsh world I lived in. That realisation has brought immense relief. I wasn't mad or stupid. I needed to be able to retreat to a place where no one could actually tell me or prove to me that I was wrong.

*

I discovered a wonderful shop filled with books about different religions and the occult, and one of my lovers bought me a crystal ball. He had shown me the pleasure of sensuality rather than mind-games sex, and making love in the forest had a lot going for it. I felt I was worshipping the gods and he was more than happy to go along with it.

As for the crystal ball, I knew I had no talent for any kind of divination. I used to keep it in a velvet pouch and it lived in my handbag and went everywhere with me. One day at work, someone had lost something and in her frustration muttered something about needing a crystal ball to find it. I took mine out of my bag and she said, 'Only you would be able to do that.' But I'm not a gypsy and no amount of wishing will make it so.

Things changed, the lover made his choices and I cast that particular crystal ball aside. It lies in the bottom of a pond among the trees. Some years later, I did buy another one and this lives in my studio. I love how the sun shines off the planes within its heart – a bit like rainbows and opals.

*

The tarot. I found a set of tarot cards all based on Greek mythology figures and I experienced a feeling of things coming together by my usual process of working out what I don't want, what is not right for me. I knew instinctively I had no special link to tarot cards. I still have them and I could set them out in a spread as I used to years ago and I could read from the book the possible meanings, but I have not ever felt the need to learn each card and its meaning. I liked doing it because it made me aware of how people think, feel and respond.

I was made aware too of the responsibility that came with the cards. Regardless of how things turned out, I didn't want to do a spread and find someone had taken meanings literally and applied them to their lives. There was one more important aspect too. I worked with a woman who consulted her tarot cards every day and wouldn't make a decision without first checking what the cards said. I knew that was not for me.

*

Viking rune stones. I loved the feel of them. I loved a sense of connection to those pagans of old. I learned that runes weren't just used by Vikings, they were a common form of divination. But again, I didn't learn the symbols and meanings by heart. I was happy to consult them the way I did the tarot cards. Part of the connection was discovering the symbols were letters of the alphabet and similar to those we use today.

*

The colour oracle. Here was another awareness. I didn't consult the oracle but every morning while I had a shower I thought about what colour I felt like that day. I chose very carefully – coordination was very important too. I matched scarves with particular outfits, and so started my collection of many scarves. Gradually, I learned what the different colours represented, how each made me feel. One of those little things that was actually supported by some research was, don't wear red when in a public place, like being on the front counter of DSS. Red is a colour of energy and strength but disastrous if you are in a situation where tempers are likely to run high and be unpredictable. Many hospital walls are painted green because it is a colour that soothes, calms and aids healing. It is a fascinating subject.

I find it intriguing that today I don't do it, at least not with the intensity and absorption I used to. Colours and clothes, they were my protection from the rest of the world. These days, I don't need to do it the same way. Yes, it's true that there are days when I make a deliberate choice to wear red, green or blue, but I know I have changed.

*

The visual I Ching. This was something new to me when I came across it. I don't have the proper coins for it but, for me, I have something more precious. Many years ago, my mother gave me a purse of hers with her initials embossed on it. We always laugh over the fact that her initials are ME for Mildred Eldridge and she thought it looked so silly. In keeping with tradition, inside was a piece of string and a silver coin.

The reason for the coin was easy to link to wishing me good fortune but I have forgotten why the piece of string. I have tried looking it up on the internet but couldn't find anything.

The coin was a silver threepenny piece from Victorian times. I decided to use the coin for the I Ching and went to an old coin shop and bought two more of similar vintage. I have not really grasped I Ching. I was interested in how it worked with the heads and tails of the coins forming symbols, but I found the explanations for those symbols rather obscure.

*

From the North American First Nation peoples I have a set of spirit stones and a set of cards *A Voice From the Earth*. I haven't used them for long years, but I have just taken them out of the small chest I use to keep all my cards and stones in and the memories of when I did consult them came back with such a warmth.

*

Gypsy dice. Three small dice in a brightly coloured crocheted bag and a little homemade booklet. You throw the dice, add up the up-facing sides and then check the meaning of that number in the book. I forgot I have them, it's been so long since I used them. There were days when I did find encouragement from them.

*

I mentioned the small chest I keep all my stones and cards in. It sits under my art desk in my studio. It's like a Davy Jones's locker treasure chest and I've just realised that it is sacred to me. Each set of cards or stones has its own individual bag that I have mostly made myself. There are some sprigs of lavender just loose in there and small amounts of sheep fleece that I have brought back from England, Wales, the Netherlands and Scotland.

*

There are three sets of cards that I do still use quite often. I write down their messages and they always help me find understanding for my responses to what someone has said to me or situations I have found myself in.

The Flower Messages. These are based on English flowers and before I even look at interpretations, I am encouraged simply because I am an English flower child. I like to read what is on a card I blindly select. Closely linked to them is a little volume called *Language of the Flowers.* Many years ago, I took myself off to Adelaide one day, for some time alone. I bought a day-tripper bus ticket and had $10 in my purse. I saw *Language of the Flowers.* It was $9.95. I can safely say my last dollar will always go on a book. No lunch for me that day!

The inscription says 'To Mother from Father' and is dated August 1913. It is a handwritten list of flowers in alphabetical order and their meaning. There are many little illustrations throughout. It has been reproduced in heavy gloss paper and a hard cover.

The only one I disagree with is his meaning of begonias. I do so love begonias but the author says they were for dark thoughts and that just doesn't work for me. But then I don't believe any flower has a truly negative meaning. I have seen any number of books with this theme but nothing quite like this one. It is a treasure indeed – with the complete collection of the Flower Fairies Stephen gave me.

The Druid Animal Oracle Deck. I am happy to be thought a pagan. I seriously wondered about the Druids and bought several books about them, but I got to the part about casting spells and I knew this wasn't for me. This deck of cards is challenging in that the illustrations are not the best. There is a fine line between a realistic representation of a bird or animal and something hinting at a Walt Disney look. Walt finds his way in a bit too much for my taste but, having said that, I find the meanings of the animals fascinating.

Animal Dreaming cards. These I found in Darwin. There is no ambiguity about the pictures, they are quite childlike and simple. Again, it is their meanings that interest me.

*

So here I am with more than one foot in a mystical world beyond logic and reason, and based entirely on my own instincts. I have said that my last dollar will go on a book but it wasn't always so. I relied heavily on the public library to assuage my hunger for knowledge.

Novels I found a satisfying way of learning English history. Within them, I also needed to have a heroine who, despite the odds, was strong enough to be true to herself. I looked to this for an example of possible ways to respond to my own difficult situation. It's interesting that I have stopped reading these books because I am my own heroine now and I have written my own book.

But books have been such wonderful travel companions.

The Merlin trilogy by Mary Stewart. This will ever be one of my favourites. The power plays with the underlying enchantment. A small thing in the opening pages of the first volume, the child Merlin looked at the apple his uncle had given him. It looked perfect, but inside its heart he could see the darkness. He dropped the apple and a bee landed on it, started tasting its sweetness and fell down dead. It was enough to grab my attention to illustrate that things are rarely what they appear to be at first glance, and so it is with people.

Years ago, I started to read a four-book series about Boudicca. I can't remember why now, but I only read the first two. In the past couple of years, I was made aware of them again, and I read all four as ebooks. There were links to a couple of books by Barbara Erskine set in the same period. Zimmer-Bradley took me back to ancient Britain in several of her books set when the Romans and Christianity had crept in and started driving pagan worship underground.

I had been introduced to Tolkien's *Hobbit* and *Lord of the Rings* by the Jesuits in my twenties but it wasn't till I reread them many years later that I learned to love them. Assisted of course by the films. It's not often that a film made from a book works for me – usually, one or the other disappoints – but Peter Jackson did a wonderful job as far as I was concerned and his visuals enhanced my imagination a hundred-fold.

Harry Potter attracted me too, both the books and the movies. There was only one I found tedious but it was an important part of the whole story.

Tolkien and Rowling showed the never-ending saga of the fight between good and evil, the light and the dark. How easy it is to be enticed down the dark path with the promise of something to satisfy our human weaknesses.

The Never-ending Story. Years ago, there was a movie made of the *Never-ending Story*. When I think about it, I am surprised my ex-husband took us to see it. In later years, I located the book but it didn't hold the same enchantment.

When my boys were in their teens, a whole raft of movies came out in quick succession, all showing that life wasn't quite as ordinary as our daily lives would have us believe. The *Superman* movies, the *Battlestar Galactica* series, *Star Trek*…all challenged our imagination. Sometimes, he did get it right.

Links

I know I am moving backwards and forwards in time but I don't know how else to put the different threads into the tapestry. It is linear but I am adding more strands to the depth and breadth of my learning.

Back to the two-day study course. I am beginning to realise how big an impact it had on me. There were only small glimpses of things, but they have stayed in one form or another.

I had been vaguely familiar with Freud and his perspective that a lot of mankind's troubles are sexually based. Carl Jung walked a similar path with him for a while, but he went off on another trajectory and developed his theory that mankind is driven by spirituality.

I was introduced to Jung and his theory of archetypes, the collective consciousness and mandalas. It made me aware that these things existed, and I had instant connection with them, but it was not until after my son died about ten years later that I was able to learn more.

In the terrible days after my son died, I looked to nature for healing. I was questioning my standards and values, but I also made sure every day that I saw one new thing that was a small wonder. The play of light and shadows, raindrops, bark on trees… I started writing poetry to make it real. I became reacquainted with the passing of seasons.

I found myself starting to be conscious of the moon. She was the perfect reflection of nature, constant yet ever changing. I was enchanted by her phases, her changing hues but without the harsh brightness of the sun's glare. She was my lifeline to enable me to function every day and keep my sanity. I had a strong need to pray, to give thanks and seek courage to continue, and where better to send my prayers than to the moon?

Much healing has come through mandalas. I have lost count of the times I have done this, mostly as paintings and a couple of times making an actual model. What are mandalas for? For me, it was and still is a way of gathering together the things that are significant to me. I am a child of nature and inevitably this is where I turn for reminders of the constancy and the changes.

I read somewhere of the universal energy of love. I consciously connect with this energy every day in the shower. I simply liked the idea that somewhere directly above me is a clear pure light. I had been reading about chakras and this was like an extra chakra above me but aligned with all the others.

The link with having a shower is the symbolism of the water being the universal energy washing away not just my fears, angst and terrors, but those of all who are in the dark, of whom there are so many, down into the earth, where they may become something beautiful like flowers in the desert and coral in the sea. I need to feel I have removed those feelings out of me and put them somewhere else, but it was important that they be transformed into something positive.

One of the important aspects of healing in this particular way has been when I have been hurt and angered by someone in particular, and, rather than hold onto those negative feelings, I needed to pray for help for the one who had hurt me.

There are some certainties in my life that only I know and there is nothing anyone else can do or say to change that. I know there is a place within that I have fallen to and I can go no lower. It is a place of absolute certainty. Just as I don't fear death, I do not fear going down to those personal depths.

When I was charged with using my grief to spoil other people's fun, I was stunned. I had only ever been shown respect as a grieving mother. However, there was some accuracy in the charge and I had to face it within myself. I know I have been freed from the restrictions of grieving mother. With the help of the universal energy of love, I could also let go of the hurt and anger towards the one who said this. I am thankful that they helped me become free but…I am ever wary.

When I lived alone, I spent a lot of time being aware of chakras, energy fields in our bodies, reiki. I remember calling to the four winds to give thanks for the things they brought into my life. Without the corrosive angst on a daily basis, the need for this has changed since I was gifted a new life with the coming of Stephen.

*

As a published poet and essayist, I have had to face the stark reality that only a handful of people will read my work. I am a compulsive writer. As I've said so often, I write to make things real. Jung to the rescue again. I choose to believe my words go to the collective unconsciousness and are accessible to anyone who looks. I will never know who has benefited from them but that doesn't matter any more.

*

I have always felt grounded to the earth. Trees and flowers are like brothers and sisters to me. I have felt very real connections with the earth in certain places. The earliest was in a certain dell in Roundhead Wood just across the lane from the old farmhouse. I could sit in there and be transported – I know not where.

In my mid-thirties, I felt it in the natural bush in the Adelaide Hills. I was perfectly attuned to the elements, felt no fear of snakes or spiders. It was the certainty that nothing could hurt me and it didn't.

In my early forties, I went to England to visit my mother, and during that holiday, my young brother took me to Wales to stay a couple of nights with Rob, a friend who used to live in our home village. Rob took me out one day and we climbed a small mountain and looked for miles along the south-western coast of Wales. I felt a tingling link to the earth at the top of that mountain. It happened again when he took me to see some standing stones. I reached out and touched one and it tingled beneath my hand.

There is one more link with the earth. I have had no wish to buy a house or own land. As it turned out, I do own a piece of land here in

Australia. As I have said, my son wished to be buried. It fell to me to organise his funeral and so his plot is in my name.

*

I am no swimmer but over the past thirty years I have a very strong connection with the sea. I have spent hours plodding along the waterline in all weathers in all seasons – always alone. I remember probably nearly forty years ago when I had a day off work and I went out to 'sink or swim' – quite literally. I knew I could float – that was one thing I managed when at high school before being turned out of the water as I was so cold. I needed to know if I could float in the sea and, better yet, could I swim?

It is such a clear memory when I let my feet leave the ocean floor and I lay with arms and legs spread. I was floating. Gradually over time I taught myself to swim mostly underwater. I still haven't managed to coordinate my breathing properly, but I am content to swim a little and float a little. The best time is after breakfast when I can watch both the sun and the moon in the sky at the same time.

I also realised if I am in the water at nearby Semaphore, then I am connected with the rest of the world. This bit of water is part of the great oceans, and of all the rivers that flow into the oceans everywhere.

I love the sunlight. Perhaps that is the real reason I am meant to be living in Australia. I am one of those people who get very low when cloudy days go on for too long. I don't much like the extreme heat, but I do need clear skies to keep my spirit light.

I love the cold, wet and windy days too. There is something invigorating about the buffeting winds, especially when walking along the waterline at the beach in the winter. Those days are the best, because there are never many people there walking their dogs.

I love watching clouds coming across the gulf, so many different moods – especially living here beside the tidal reach called the Port River. I love the purity of the blue sky, those glimpses of eternity that brings some relief when it is cloudy. Even this little stretch of water has so many moods and is never still. It is better than living beside a river as I did in the hills in my tree house. There, the water was only going one way – to meet up with the sea. The tidal reach, on the other hand, ebbs and flows and I am reminded of that as I write because I am going backwards and forwards finding strands that need to be woven in.

I don't have a favourite mood for the tidal reach. I love the absolute stillness we wake to most mornings when the pink sky is reflected like a mirror. I love the blue/green of a sunny day. I love it when there is a king tide and the wind is strong enough to push the water more and more until it breaks the banks. It is like a wide animal and I have often written about it.

I love rainbows. I love the idea that they are connecting the heavens with the earth. When I emigrated fifty-something years ago, I saw a rainbow from the plane. It was a perfect circle.

When we were in Scotland a few years ago, I recognised that only the bottom of my feet were on the ground, that the rest of me was in the 'sky'.

*

I have not been brave when it comes to looking at the night sky. I have written about the sun, the Great Spirit, who is too hard and bright, but vital to life on the planet. It took the death of my son to give me the courage to look at the night sky. I read somewhere about stars being linked by music. A fantasy perhaps but one that I connected to instantly.

Some say that the stars are our loved ones who have left this life. I haven't been able to embrace the idea. Do I know why? The logic I said I was going to keep out of this as much as possible.

I've tried to see the different constellations and feel I have not succeeded at all. My eldest son has tried on several occasions – even the night we were lying on the lawn watching Halley's comet going over. I said yes I can see the tail but I don't know if I did or not. I have watched a movie called *Contact* many times. It touches on time and distance in outer space. A whole different concept. Logic says it was clever special effects but I don't care. What it did was stretch my mind to the concept of endless, no-edges distance. I have learned to accept that there are some things in my life that my mind cannot get to the edges of. When I am confronted with them, I can only acknowledge they are there and let quiet ease my angst. So it is with the universe.

I have an app on my computer that shows me the night sky as it is at any moment. I love to look at what planets are in our neighbourhood. I greet them like family members. I recall when we took the Indian Pacific train from Adelaide to Sydney. I curled up in my cabin and watched for hours and hours the night sky facing south. I didn't see any artificial lights. I was being watched by two very bright stars the whole time. It was the most wonderful connection possible.

*

Going back to mandalas for a moment. I have taken this a step or two beyond painting a picture or creating a model of an idea. I have used tattoos to write my own mandala on my skin. Unlike a lot of people today, my tattoos are hidden from view. I have trouble with the whole 'sleeve' look wherever it's placed on the body. For the Maori people, their tattoos have a specific meaning and are very individual. This craze I see everywhere for lots of tattoos often looks like someone is trying to hide who they really are.

So why do I have them and why do I keep them hidden? I wanted the first one to remind me of my dead son. I designed a candle flame that is on the top of my right shoulder. All those times I have embraced myself, I am mindful of the flame. At the time, it was unusual to have coloured images. My flame is yellows and reds and has no blue outline. The man who did it for me was concerned. He said a lot of public places wouldn't allow you in if you had such a tattoo on display. My goodness, how things have changed. The flame also represented the obvious – fire.

Water is the symbol of emotions. I was in a relationship at one time and I had a name inked on my leg – high so it was not on display.

Choices were made and it became inappropriate for it to remain there unchanged. It is unchanged of course, but I have had another symbol inked over it – a seal. It was supposed to be a young one but the tattoo artist didn't do a very good job of it. Somehow that was very significant at the time. Seals always look as if they are weeping. It is relevant for many reasons.

Time passed and I decided to get a moth inked close to the flame. It represents the air. It is also love being ever drawn like a moth to a flame, and I have not been afraid to love in this life.

The fourth tattoo is also one I designed to represent the earth. I didn't fancy a mountain, so have oak leaves and a couple of acorns. It is in autumn colours of bronze and gold. The last one I had done in more recent years and summed up everything else. A crescent moon and some falling stars holds within it the moth and the flame.

Sometimes I wonder about another one, but what would I have? I have the symbols of fire, air earth and water. And the moon.

Cultures

I do have trouble with my English background when I think about the atrocities the British have performed in the name of the Empire. In their arrogance, they have insisted that their way is the only way to do things and demolished anything that didn't conform.

I talk of climbing up on my English dignity and I know I do it, as if I am better than others. I watch British films or TV series and the quality cannot be denied. I can remember Mother used to say, 'You are my daughter, as good as anyone and better than most.' And she truly meant it with no intended arrogance, just a certainty in what she was saying.

Over the years, I've tried to console myself that I am a child of the universe but I'm not sure I have convinced myself.

When I was nineteen/twenty and living in Dublin for almost a year, I felt keenly the hatred of the Irish towards the English – for, I freely admit, very good reasons. Something in me is still drawn to Ireland. My children's father is Irish. He told me all Irishmen are connected to the five kings of Ireland from way back and he was a descendent of the kings of Leinster. I wanted to believe him and, I realise now, I did.

I love Irish music. They have a particular way of being in the world that I feel drawn to, admire and at the same time am frustrated by. I have tried to delve into their mythology but have not been able to make a connection. Yet when I read of the Druids in the Boudicca stories and the notion that many of them escaped to Ireland before the Romans slaughtered those left on the Isle of Mona, I feel this vibration of 'Yes'.

I have read a little about the Tuatha De Danaan, a supernatural tribe who, with the arrival of Christianity, went to live in the underworld. I wonder if perhaps it's time to pursue that now.

When we visited Scotland a few years ago, the legacy of the Clearances and the treatment of the Scots by the English made me cringe. But I was given a gift. Out in the mountains, away from the tour group we were with and instead spending a few precious hours with my brother, I heard voices on the wind. Glencoe is a tragic part of Scottish history and I could hear those women weeping and grieving for lost fathers, husbands, brothers and sons.

This brings me to Australia and the Ancient Ones here. When I started work at DSS, I was at the Salisbury office. I knew nothing of the Aboriginal people who had inhabited this land for thousands of years. My first experience of them was at the front counter of DSS. It was probably one of the worst places to meet them. Someone explained to me that they did not make eye contact. I found this challenging because I relied heavily on eye contact to make a connection with someone. It had proved effective in this environment. The other difficulty I had was that they seemed to often come in the worse for alcohol and, as I've already written, this made me wary of unpredictable behaviour, Not a good start.

My third son has two sons, now in their twenties. Their mother is part-Aboriginal. It was one of those incongruities that she had Irish blood in her too which showed in her reddish-blonde hair and her green eyes.

I welcomed these two newborn grandsons with the knowledge that they linked me to this land more than anything had before. The relationship was a hazardous one and when she assaulted him, Community Welfare stepped in and took the two boys from her and gave them to their father, my son. What happened to my son is not something I want to dwell on. Suffice it to say he escaped with badly damaged vision in one eye. But he has done a marvellous job raising his children. Neither of them appear to have any interest in their Aboriginal heritage and, with their blond hair and blue eyes, it isn't obvious in them.

*

Windows of opportunity opened up for me with the new life that came with Stephen. Travelling from top to bottom and side to side of this country, I have felt the presence of the Ancient Ones.

It was in Darwin that I learned a different awareness of plight of Aboriginal people. Walking in the town, we saw elders sitting on the pavements. I unwittingly made eye contact with one as we passed. So much pain and loss.

One evening we sat on the lawns in front of our hotel to eat fish and chips as we watched the sunset. To one side of us were a group of keep-fit enthusiasts with their loud music and raised voices giving instructions for the exercises they were doing. To the other side of us were a group of Aboriginal people who were drunk but not doing any harm to anyone. The police pulled up and ignored the keep-fit group and started trying to move on the Aboriginals. One voice cried out, 'This is my land.' In that voice was immeasurable pain and loss. I was frustrated by the inequality that was being demonstrated.

I am aware of my own conflicting emotions. The Aboriginal people say quite rightly this is their land. We have taken everything from them and left them no clear means of identity. Yet some leave litter and detritus everywhere they go. I want to say, 'Clear up this mess and show how important this land is to you.' As a people, I know many are lost to their traditional ways. With losses of my own that cannot be undone, so I see this echoed in their eyes.

My experiences with the Ancient Ones have been wonderful. Walking among the trees in Tasmania, I felt the little hand of a girl in mine. I felt the presence of her family close by. I felt the elder in the Dismal Swamp. At Hay, in New South Wales, I felt the warmth and laughter of the Auntie in our motel room and when we drove away I heard the shrieks of laughter of children playing in the creek.

I have been interested in their Dreamtime stories but I get tangled up with translations and the different tribes each with their own but similar legends and myths. As yet, it isn't a world I have attempted to explore – other than through one of several original Aboriginal paintings we have hanging on our walls. It is a large canvas depicting the night sky with the Milky Way centrally placed. Over it is a whale and the Seven Sisters. There is a full moon in one corner and diagonally across is the Earth, which interestingly shows Australia as the land mass to identify it, not the usual Europe, Africa or Americas. I have a book about the story of the Seven Sisters but for some reason I have been unable to explain, I have not done anything more than glance at its contents. Part of my problem is that Aboriginal history is an oral one. I know they had a pictorial language to leave messages for other tribe members to follow, but they had no written language.

White man came here and destroyed so much but there were a few who did try and learn from the Indigenous people but I wonder how carefully or accurately the stories were recorded and translated. I learned only recently that it was German missionaries who helped develop an Aboriginal alphabet so their language could be written down and read.

Home Studies and Ginninderra Press

Since being with Stephen, my reading has expanded enormously. He has encouraged my thirst for knowledge. He bought me the complete Greek tragedies. It was staggering stuff. As I have said before, it was like coming home. Written all those centuries ago, yet the people were no different from how we are today. Basic human nature hasn't changed. I find that incredibly comforting.

How rich I am to have my own personal library now. Stephen and I had talked about my longing to go to university and when I retired from public service at sixty, it was my opportunity. I had done an entry exam years previously so I knew I had a place if I wanted it. But it was interesting to discover that I really didn't want to write essays from set reading to prove to someone I could do that. I needed something far more open and flowing. Stephen became my tutor.

Stephen has opened up another world for me – as an editor, working with him in Ginninderra Press. Our 'working day' ends at four in the afternoon and we gravitate to the cosy corner downstairs with its large windows overlooking the tidal reach. This is my study time and place. It is perfect.

I can't really say what the best thing about this arrangement is. Partly it is reading something and being able to ask a question without fear of criticism or censure. Stephen might offer me his opinion or he will wander to the bookshelves of his extensive library and find a volume that he will hand to me with the casual comment that I might find it interesting. The wonderful thing about this is, he doesn't get offended if I choose not to read it or to read only some of what he has offered. On the internet and whenever we visit a bookshop, he is always on the lookout for books he think will interest me .

Stephen also understands and embraces my need for escapism at times and never makes me feel uncomfortable about it. He might not be a fan of Harry Potter or Tolkien but he did come with me to the cinema to see the new films when they came out.

It is a two-way street, though, because I have watched many, many films with him that there is no way I would have gone anywhere near on my own – especially those of Hitchcock. I remember saying years ago that I'm not afraid of anything in my head, but at the same time I refuse to put images of ugliness of any kind in there. Violence might be part of a storyline but I simply shut my eyes. It's the same with films that show anyone playing with another mind. It is a path I have been dragged down and I will not ever allow it to happen to me again.

What started out as a love of Greek mythology has developed into a deep interest in ancient times, how civilisations developed and how they influence our world today. I am currently reading about the Persians. So much of who we are in Western culture today has come down from them from over two and a half thousand years ago.

There is a trend these days for novels written by women about the female figures in Greek history and mythologies. Perhaps it's because I have read so much about them that each new book seems to overlap others and I am joining the dots to make a richer picture.

I have just finished reading a very new book called *Elektra* by Jennifer Saint. On my bookshelf I have the play *Electra* by Euripides, translated by Gilbert Murray. Yes, of course the story is essentially the same – no doubt Jennifer Saint used the play as one of her sources – but as a woman she has brought the character of Elektra so richly to life. Again, it's that fundamental fact that people haven't changed much in centuries.

*

To return to a short throwaway sentence from earlier: Stephen has opened up another world for me – as an editor, working with him in Ginninderra Press.

Never in my wildest dreams did I ever imagine I would become part of a publishing house. I'm not even sure if that is the correct term to use. Stephen is a sole trader, publishing books as Ginninderra Press.

We had been together for a year when the time was right for me to retire from the public service. All those compulsory superannuation deductions I had made for twenty-five years now ensure that I have some capital savings as a cushion against financial hardship, and a fortnightly pension. Our very modest income from the business still means we are entitled to age pensions. We are comfortable enough. One day, our landlord might sell the hosue we live in or we will stop running the business and we will have to move. Meanwhile, we treasure every moment we live here.

Travel has been an important part of our lives. How blessed we are to have authors from all over Australia, which has meant we have travelled to book launches and events in all states but Western Australia and the Northern Territory. Sadly, since Covid, our travels have been curtailed and we miss the real-life interaction with our authors.

For a few weeks after I retired, I did nothing. I hadn't realised how tired I was, but it didn't take long before I was bored and wanted something to do. I turned to Stephen. He introduced me to the preparation and layout work required when he has accepted a manuscript for publication and has received the electronic version.

I was having great fun. These were the days when all sorts of weird charcaters – wingdings! – appeared among the text. Things have changed even in ten years and I don't get those any more. The process of putting the text into a template was far simpler than I would have believed. Not only were my computer skills expanding, so was my exposure to poetry in particular.

Stephen publishes poetry, short stories, novels and non-fiction. Suddenly I was reading things I know I would not have done in any other circumstance.

I learned to discern the anxious ones who had little confidence in themselves as people and as poets. Knowing what it meant to be a published poet, I found it exciting that I was part of changing someone's life in ways they couldn't have anticipated. It was one of the things Stephen acknowledged publicly in our early days. He was seeing first hand the difference being published made to a person's life. He found it disconcerting that he was being written in to all of my work.

The wind of change always likes to blow and it came past me in a big way in late 2014. After some enquiries by poets and a lot of thought, Stephen decided he would start a series of chapbooks called Pocket Poets. He wanted me to be the editor. That was huge! The series was open only to poets previously published by Ginninderra Press, so I was on safe ground, as they had already proven the quality of their poetry.

2015 came and the owner of Picaro Press was having to retire because of ill health. Stephen took over the name and some of their titles. He decided to start a series of chapbooks called Picaro Poets and opened them to anyone living in Australia. I was to be their editor. This was a much bigger challenge because I was the one saying yes or no to poetry submissions. Hundreds of titles later, both series are still going strong. We have sold well over 25,000 of them.

I love the email link I have with the poets. I love how a poet changes when I have said yes to publishing.

In 2019, we decided to start a poetry journal called *The Crow*. I knew I didn't want to be editor so we invited our friend Joan Fenney to take on the task. When she stepped down after two years, I agreed to take her place. It hasn't been as stressful as I feared. I developed my own administrative side of it to suit me and so far it is working.

My days are full and there are times when I get weary of words. There are times when I want to do my own writing and I am thankful that I have no restrictions placed on me at all.

Who am I?

Today at seventy-two, I can say with absolutely sincerity that I have had an amazing life and I give thanks for it every single day.

For a long time, I was too close to tragedy and heartache to be able to see that saying, 'I will have what is right for me, when it is right for me' wasn't just something I was saying to convince myself of it, I was in fact living it.

It was a process of elimination. When a situation was no longer right for me, I said no and moved on. To write that sentence was simple. The harsh reality of living that philosophy was exactly that – harsh reality. I often bemoaned that if something was right then why was it so hard to do. The answer was that to continue to do the wrong thing was worse.

When I was fifty-nine, I made the decision that I wanted to live my life differently. I wanted to grow into myself.

Have I become the wise woman sitting in the wisdom chair in the desert? Yes and no.

Have I been living in the desert? No.

I had to think about that carefully. I admit there are things in my life that I wouldn't put my hand up for to experience but when thrust upon me I had to choose how I was going to respond. And I have responded by finding the positives wherever I could, and they were always there if I looked hard enough, long enough. I have not ever had 'nothing' and I say that in light of the definition of a desert being a place where nothing grows.

*

Subconsciously, I thought a wise woman lived in a village, a little separate from the village centre. She would have a garden filled with flowers and herbs and birds, surrounded by a high hedge to keep out prying eyes. Folks would go to her when they needed help with illness or troubles in hearth and home. She was a go-to person.

When I was still with my ex-husband and our children, I was part of a community. I knew my neighbours and their children. When I left, I didn't ever again become part of a neighbourhood in the same way. My home was my haven from the rest of the world and I didn't want anyone in it except by specific invitation. I needed to protect myself at all costs.

During my twenty-five years in the public service, the office was my 'village' and my work colleagues the ones who sought me out. Sometimes they came to my desk when they needed help with a case they were working on. I had built my reputation with great care over the years. I also became an expert in a field no one else wanted to play in.

The tea room was my other office. Work colleagues of both sexes would come and talk to me while I made my cups of tea. The topics were mostly concerning family life. Everyone knew I was living a parents' worse nightmare of losing a child. It was interesting that I was respected because I was doing what I was doing…getting on with life as best I could every day. I always began my responses with the words, 'In that situation I did this…' or 'My mother taught me…'

It was pointed out to me once that one of the differences between men and women is that, faced with a problem, men want to fix it. Women will sit around the table with endless cups of tea and talk about it. Nothing might get resolved as such, but everyone felt better. I can see how accurate that is.

Being the go to person meant I didn't feel I could go to someone. I found my own answers in the responses to others.

*

When I retired, I wondered who would be my village. I was in uncharted territory. Stephen was treating me with a loving respect I had never known. I learned over time that I am loved because I am who I am, not in spite of who I am. I found a new way of loving with Stephen's daughter and his granddaughters (one as a little girl of almost four when I came into her life and the other as a teenager). I had no sisters, no daughters, no granddaughters and no close women friends. These females opened me to a very different way of loving.

*

One thing I quickly became aware of when we attended book launches and events was that I was mixing with other writers and there was an instant connection. It was so easy to be with strangers, sharing all sorts of pieces of information. I had always found it so easy to connect with men. Now I was connecting with women with similar ease.

As my role in Ginninderra Press expanded, so did my direct email contact with writers. It was Stephen who recognised what was happening. He said I created the Ginninderra Press family. He now says he is the head of Ginninderra Press, but I am the heart. I love this and I am warmed by his generosity.

An unlooked-for development was having my artwork and photographs used for covers of some Ginninderra Press publications. I am very pleased by this, but at the same time I feel far more exposed than with my writing.

*

There have been two other events that have set me free from the past. My ex-husband and my mother have died. I have reasons to be thankful to both of them for many things but I am relieved that they have gone.

I am no one's child. My children will always have me as their mother, but they are grown men, have made lives of their own, have children and grandchildren of their own. They don't need me.

I have been embraced by Stephen's family but they don't need me either. They know I love their father and they trust me with him. What greater gift is there?

I love being Stephen's wife but I am equally pleased that I am recognised as a writer, artist and editor – as Brenda Eldridge. The person I have been all along.

www.ingramcontent.com/pod-product-compliance
Lightning Source LLC
Chambersburg PA
CBHW030046100526
44590CB00011B/343